D0944946

Brian Wingate

Dedicated to my mom and dad, for my first bike

Published in 2003 by The Rosen Publishing Group, Inc.
29 East 21st Street, New York, NY 10010

First Edition

Library of Congress Cataloging-in-Publication Data

Wingate, Brian.
BMX bicycle racing : techniques and tricks / by Brian Wingate.— 1st ed.
p. cm. — (Rad sports)
Includes bibliographical references (p.) and index.
ISBN 0-8239-3843-3 (lib. bdg.)
1. Bicycle motocross—Juvenile literature. [1. Bicycle motocross.
2.Bicycle racing.] I. Title. II. Series.
GV1049.3 .W56 2003
796.6'2—dc21

2002005046

Manufactured in the United States of America

CONTENTS

Introduction

Do you have the need for speed? Do you ever ride your bike and wish that you could ride faster than ever before? Or find the coolest jumps and obstacles to ride over? Would you like to soar gracefully through the air? Do you ever wish you could find other people your age to ride with and even compete against? Do you dream of taking first place after a hard race? Do you like to push yourself to the limit to get your best effort? Do you love to see dirt fly out behind your bike as you pedal as hard as you can?

If you answered yes to any of these questions, there's a sport out there just for you. If the thrill of a chase, the danger of a jump, and the rush of competition all appeal to you, there's a sport that's a perfect fit. It's called bicycle motocross, or BMX. BMX is one of the most exciting sports around.There are a few things you should know before you get started. You'll have to prepare your body and your mind.

In this book, you'll learn how to buy a bike, what gear to wear, how races are run, and what to expect when you ride on a new track. But most important, you'll learn valuable tips that will help you get a head start on the competition. You'll find out how to pass other riders and how to protect your lead. And BMX can teach you the best thing of all—how to have fun.

Chapter 1

Laying the Foundation

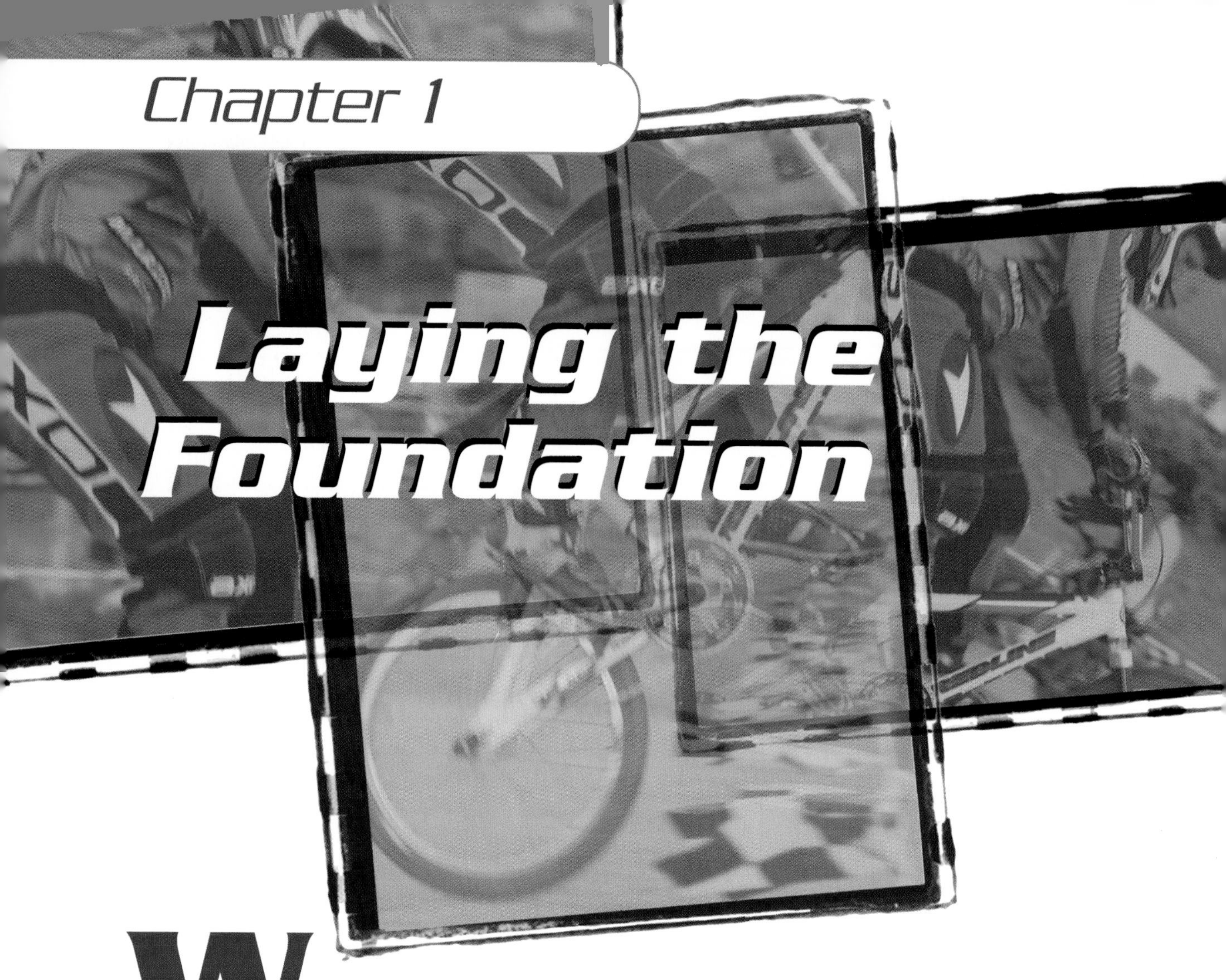

When you ride on a BMX track, it's like entering a bicycle playground. The twisting, turning dirt track is full of hills and jumps. Any BMX track is a lot of fun to look at and even more fun to ride. And as you start riding, you'll realize that it takes a lot of skill to be the best.

Anatomy of a Track

There are several types of jumps and obstacles that you will find on a BMX track. The track itself is usually outdoors, and it's made of dirt, sand, and gravel.

BMX tracks are laid out on flat ground but have jumps and turns built to test and aid the racers as they pedal around the track.

A single jump or hill is called a roller. Sometimes you will see two or three in a row—these are called doubles or triples. A step-up is another kind of jump combination. In a step-up, there is one small jump followed by a larger one. A tabletop looks like its name. You ride up one side and then there is a flat surface before you ride down the other side. Whoop-de-dos are a succession of small ridges or hills, one after another.

Most tracks are made up of these basic elements. Jumps can come in many different sizes, lengths, and heights. Every track is a new experience.

Races are often won and lost in the turns. High-backed berms help riders gain momentum, pass, or block other racers.

Twisting and Turning

BMX tracks have twisting turns, and it takes a lot of skill to keep your speed. These banked turns are called berms. Berms are angled so that riders can keep their speed throughout the turn. Berms are an important part of the racetrack because many riders try to pass each other in the turns. You can ride high up on the berm or cut the corner close. It's a shorter distance around the inside of a turn, but it's easier to keep your speed on the high side of the berm. You must think about your strategy during a race and make decisions on the fly. We'll learn a few passing techniques later in the book.

Anatomy of a Race

BMX races are all about bursts of power and speed. The average race lasts about a minute or less. WHAT? A minute or less? That's right. BMX riders ride only once around the track, and the average track is only 800 to 1,300 feet (243–396 meters) long. So it only takes about a minute to get around the track. But that's only the beginning. You don't take home the winner's trophy after only one race. There are two rounds in a BMX competition. Each race around the track is called a moto. Up to eight riders compete at the same time. The first round consists of three motos. At the end of each moto, riders are given point totals that match their finishing position. So the first-place rider gets one point, the second-place rider gets two, and the eighth-place rider gets eight points. At the end of three motos, the four riders with the fewest points advance to the second round. They race in three more motos against each other. At the end of these three motos, the rider with the fewest points is declared the winner. Riders call this "winning the main."

Unlike sports such as basketball and baseball, in BMX you want to get the fewest points. Sometimes the winners get big trophies, but the best feeling is knowing that you raced to the best of your ability.

If you're just starting to race, you don't have to worry about getting left in the dust by more experienced riders. Races are organized by age and skill level. BMX races are open to boys and girls of all ages. Some BMXers are as young as six years old!

Freestyle

When some people think of BMX, they don't think of a dirt track and a finish line. They think of bikes being balanced on their handrails and riders doing backflips in the air. They are thinking of freestyle BMX. Freestyle began when BMX racers tried doing stunts when they weren't racing. Now freestyle is a sport of its own, and it is one of the most popular of the extreme sports. You can check out freestyle riders and their tricks in magazines like *RideBMX*.

BMX bikes are specially made for racing. Every part of a BMX bike is heavy-duty so that it can take the punishment that racing and jumping puts on the vehicle.

Buying a Bike

When you're used to riding street bikes, a BMX bicycle looks like the Incredible Shrinking Bike. You'll see young kids and thirty-year-olds all riding the same small-frame bikes. There are some differences between models, but all BMX bikes are small and strong. They are built this way for speed and durability. Go down to your local bike shop to make sure your bike's frame is the right size for your body. You'll have to see what works best for you.

If you're choosing your own bike, you might also get to pick out your own wheels. Narrow wheels are good for small riders, while wider wheels are good for bigger riders because they support more weight. Wider wheels also give you more grip in the turns.

How BMX Got Started

The words "bicycle motocross" give you a big clue about the beginnings of the sport. BMX is a bicycle version of the sport of motocross racing. In the 1970s, a lot of kids loved the sport of motocross. But motocross bikes have big engines and are too dangerous for young riders. Before long, a bunch of kids in California started racing their own bikes in imitation of their motocross heroes. Bicycle companies started making tougher frames that could hold up under pressure when they saw how many kids wanted to ride BMX-style. Before long, there were contests and clubs across the country.

To get the most out of your wheels, put a slightly wider wheel in front. It will give you better traction in the turns, while the narrow back tire will power through the track. Of course, every bike must have handlebars. If you tilt your handlebars forward, you'll get more power; if you tilt them back, you'll have more control.

Pedal Power

There are several types of pedals: cage, platform, and clipless. Cages and platform pedals both work great for a BMXer of any skill level. Cage pedals are probably your best bet. They keep your feet secure, and you can remove them easily at any time. Clipless pedals are gaining in popularity, but they are not recommended for beginning riders. On clipless pedals, you actually attach your shoe to the pedal itself. You must be very familiar with the pedal to remove your foot quickly in case of a fall. Make sure you have some races under your belt before you try clipless pedals.

Chapter 2

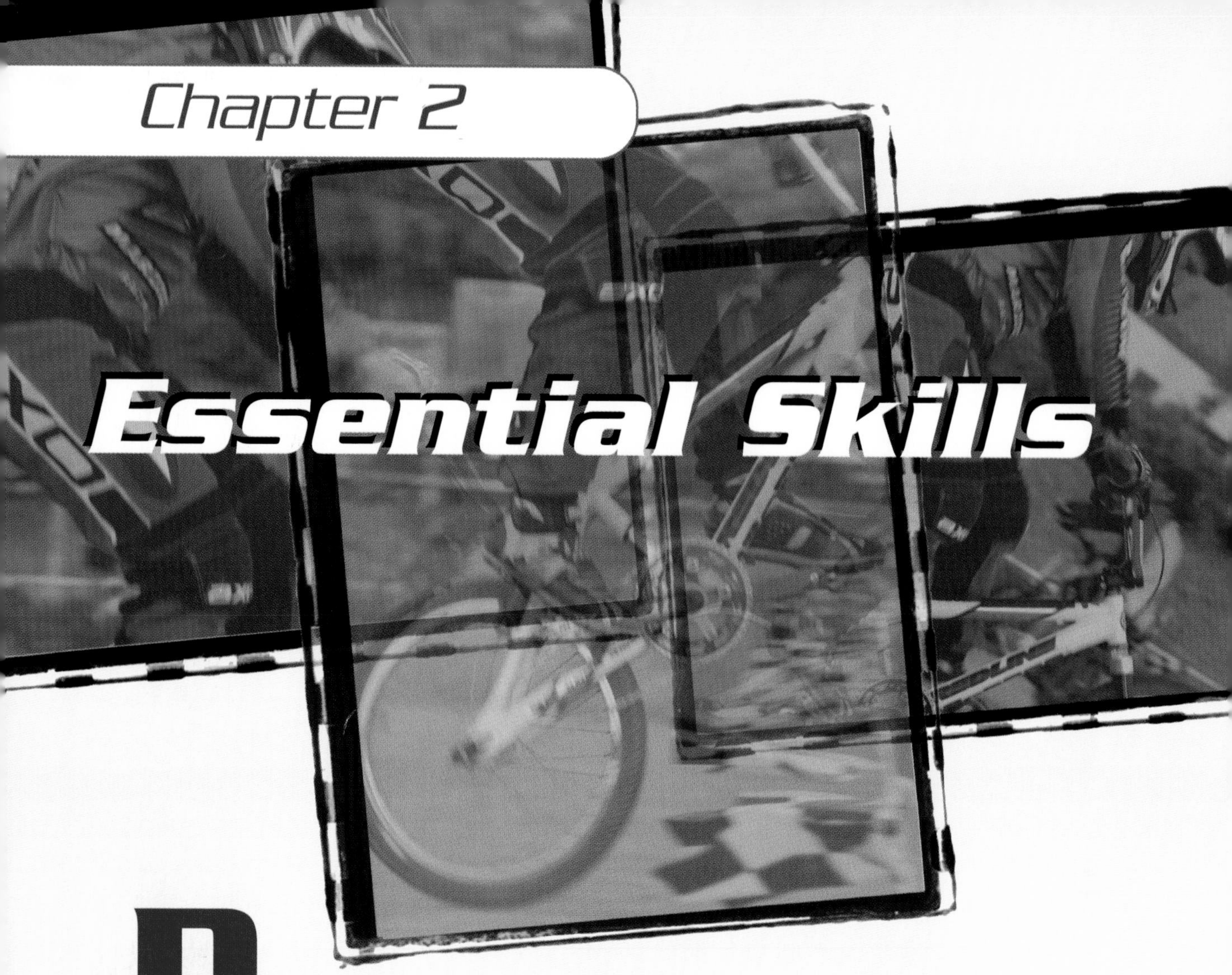

Essential Skills

Do you ever leave home without your shoes? Probably not, because they help you to get around in many situations. An experienced BMXer never leaves home without the most important tools in every racer's toolbox. You might call them the BMX riding basics. They are rolling jumps, manuals, jumping, and speed jumping.

Rolling Jumps

When you first start riding, you will probably want to take every jump at great speed and fly high into the air. First, take some time to get used to your bike, your body, and the track. A great way to do this is by rolling jumps. When you roll jumps you use the rhythm of your body to gain speed without pedaling. You roll over the jump instead of jumping over it.

1. Ride into the rolling jump with your legs loose and slightly flexed.

2. As you hit the rolling jump, let your legs flex up into your body as the bike rolls over the jump. DO NOT push off the jump.

3. As you come down the back side of the jump, push down and forward with your legs. Keep your arms and legs loose and your pedals level. Keep the wheels in contact with the ground. When you roll through several jumps in a row, you will have a smooth pumping motion.

As you get used to rolling jumps, you'll find a rhythm between your arms, your legs, and the bike. As an exercise, try to race around the entire track without pedaling. If you can do that, you will have a great understanding of how to use your body for maximum power.

Manuals

A manual is one of the best ways to practice balance and control. A manual is basically a rolling wheelie. To do a manual, start pedaling and build up some speed.

1. Shift your body weight back and pull your legs in tight.

2. Pull the handlebars up as you come to the jump.

3. As the wheel rises, push down and forward with your legs. Manuals are a great way to power up the front of a jump and dip down quickly on the jump's back side.

You can practice manuals if you pedal at a slow speed on a flat, open surface like a parking lot. Once you pop up that front wheel, try to keep rolling on your back wheel without pedaling. See how far you can go. This move will take a lot of practice and balance, so keep trying!

Jumping

Every BMXer loves to speed up a jump, launch with the legs, and fly high into the air. This is fun, but not a good idea if you want to start winning some races. The rider who learns to stay low on jumps will pass a high flyer every time. Why? Because you lose speed in the air as the wind resistance pushes against your body. Also, you aren't pedaling in the air. As anyone knows, as soon as you stop pedaling you begin to lose speed. By the time you reach the ground you have to pedal harder to catch up, and you might be eating the dirt of other riders.

1

1. When you catch a jump, pull up on the handlebars as you spring off the launch.

2

2. Try to keep the bike level in the air.

3 Jumping (continued)

3. As you land, absorb the shock of the impact with your whole body. Keep your wrists, arms, and legs loose, and use them like springs to compress as you land and keep going.

Never jump into the air directly behind another rider. If he or she crashes, you'll crash too!

Land on both wheels evenly or you may suddenly find yourself without a bike. If the front wheel lands first, you might fly over the handlebars. If the back wheel lands first, the bike may scoot out from under you, leaving you sitting on the track looking at the sky.

When you first start jumping, take some time to learn control in the air. Every jump has three elements: 1) speed, 2) a springing launch off the back of the jump, and 3) control in the air. You need all three ingredients for a successful jump. Riders with speed and a strong launch will end up eating dirt if they can't control the bike in the air. So start slow and work your way up. Get a feel for the bike and the track before you try to break any world records for air time.

Speed Jumping

Now that you've learned manuals and jumping, it's time to combine both techniques. Speed jumps allow you to power the bike over a jump and keep your highest possible speed. In a speed jump, your front tire never touches the front slope of the jump because you do a manual up the front side. You go a little faster when only your back tire touches the ground.

1. Push forward with your hips just before you reach the jump, and pull the wheel into the air.

2. Compress your body and spring up the front of the jump. Push hard with your pedals and power right up to the launch.

3. Stay low over the jump and push your bike down onto the back side of the jump.

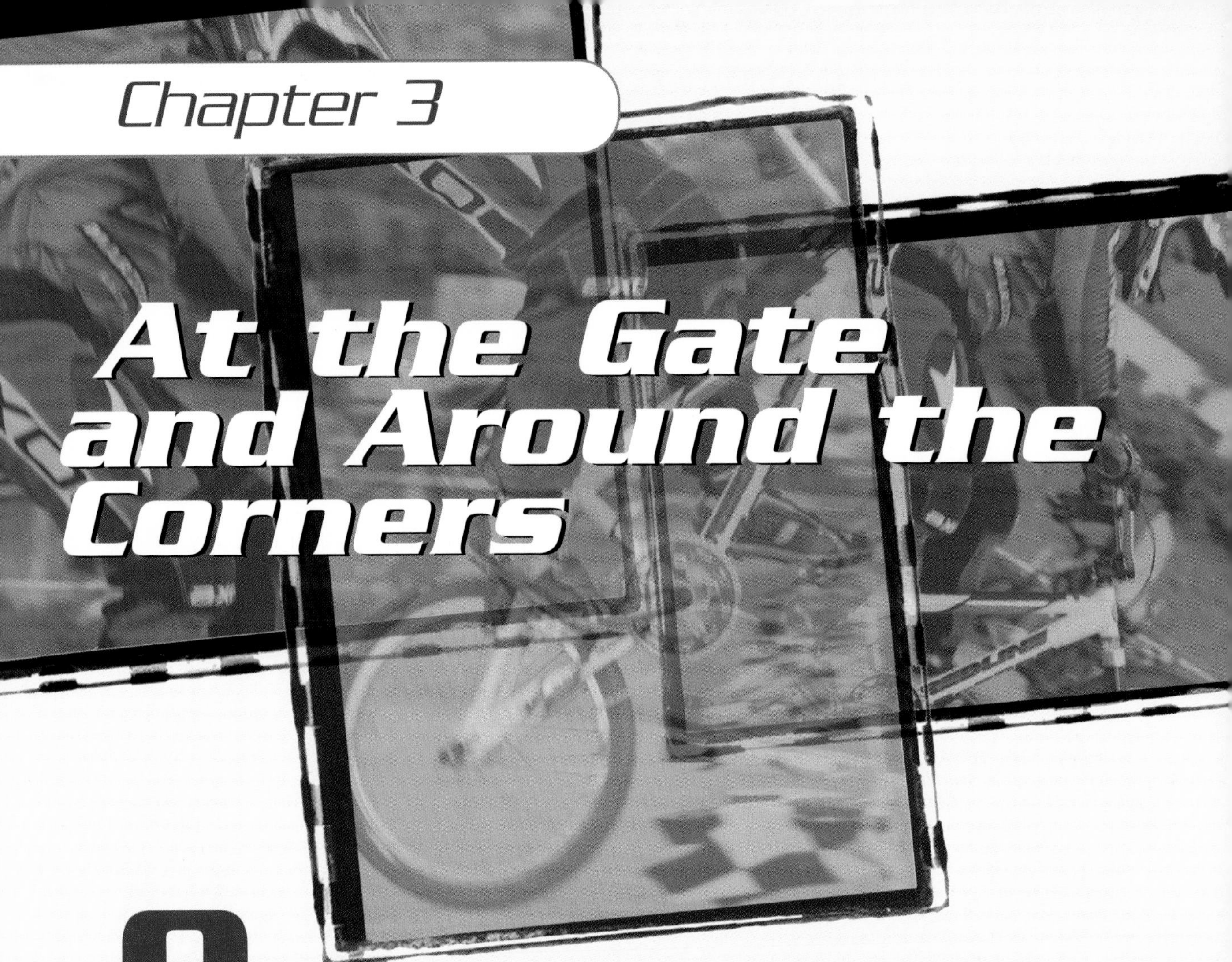

Chapter 3

At the Gate and Around the Corners

OK, it's time to get down to the nitty-gritty. You've practiced the BMX basics and now you're ready to race. Let's learn how to master some racing secrets.

Don't Sit Tight

When you're sitting at the starting gate, take a moment and say good-bye to your seat. You won't be sitting during the race. Sitting down in a BMX race is like driving a go-cart on a NASCAR track: you'll get passed every time. So stay crouched in the air above your seat. Think of yourself slicing through the air and speeding toward the finish line. During a race you won't sit on your seat very much, but hopefully it will come in handy when you raise your arms on a victory lap after winning the main.

Gate Starts

Gate starts are one of the most important parts of a race. You need to constantly practice gate starts to succeed in BMX racing. If you can get a strong start out of the gate, you automatically have a head start on the competition. The first rider through the first turn often wins the race, so there are many important factors that go into a successful start.

Balancing at the Gate

Just before a race begins, all the riders are lined up at the gate and ready for action. The countdown begins: Three, two, one, go! The starting gate is lowered, and everyone takes off in a blaze of speed and a spray of dirt. Some riders immediately shoot out ahead of the pack, while others are left behind. How can you fly out of the gate? Let's look at a good start step-by-step.

The first secret to a fast start is to balance against the starting gate. Some riders sit at the starting gate with one foot on the ground for balance, but you'll see others perched on their pedals and ready to fly when the starting buzzer sounds. It will take some practice, but you can learn to balance against the gate. You can practice at home with your front wheel against a wall.

1. Keep your pedals level and push slightly against the wall.

Balancing at the Gate (continued)

2. Keep your body weight still and balanced over your pedals.

3. Twist the handlebars to keep steady. By moving the handlebars back and forth, you can learn to balance without touching your feet to the ground. If it's hard at first, don't worry! Your body is learning a new skill. You'll get it with practice.

Posture and Foot Positions

There are a few more secrets that will help you to get the most out of your start. Once you learn to balance, you can focus on your posture and positioning.

1. Stay straight in the gate and keep your pedals level. Many bikers turn their bikes just slightly toward their front pedal for more power. So if your right pedal is in front, angle your bike slightly to the right.

2. Keep your front foot flat on the pedal and make sure both legs are slightly bent.

3. Lean your upper body back until you can feel a slight stretch in the muscle under your arm. Your arms should be straight with your wrists rolled forward slightly.

Once you feel like you're in position, look down briefly at your seat. You should be able to see half of your seat between your legs. If you see the whole seat, you're too far back; and if you don't see it at all, you're too far forward. Now look up and keep your eyes focused on the track ahead. Let your body balance itself and let your eyes figure out the track.

The Snap

The starting bell sounds, and it's time to spring into action! It's time to learn how to "snap" into motion and fly around that first turn before the other riders have a chance to catch their breath.

1. When the bell sounds, drive your front foot down and your hips forward.

2. As the gate drops, pull up with your back foot while throwing the bike out with your hips. If you time it right, your bike will lunge forward just as the gate hits the ground.

Snap Secrets

Experienced riders make it look simple, but there are many ingredients in the perfect start. You want to learn the right way now, when you're a beginner, so you won't have to erase bad habits later on.

To come out of that gate like a pro, remember that your starting power is in your hips. When you lunge forward, your hips are supplying the power that moves the bike forward.

When you see good riders come out of the gate you will notice that their front wheel rises off the ground and into the air. The force of their hips and legs pushing forward causes this, not their arms. Many beginning riders pull up on their front handlebars in an attempt to pop that front wheel into the air. If you lift the handlebars, your body will lose its forward momentum.

The best way to perfect your starting technique is to watch the best riders in action. Go out to the track and watch other riders come out of the gate. Is there one rider who always seems to come first out of the gate? Study his or her technique, and even ask for advice. You'll be glad you did.

Break away from the pack by pedaling hard and rolling jumps instead of launching into the air. Your speed and momentum can carry you to an easy victory.

Breaking Away from the Pack

Once you're out of the gate, you don't always find yourself in the lead. Sometimes you'll find yourself in the middle of the pack. This is hard because the riders on all sides limit your moves. But you want to be in front where the track is yours and it's clear sailing to the finish line! When you're in the middle of the pack, you want to look for ways to break into the lead while preventing others from passing you. Keep your elbows out to protect yourself, but be careful not to elbow other riders. Throwing elbows is a quick way to get disqualified from a race. Try to surge ahead in a turn and move your bike in the path of other riders so they can't pass you. We'll learn some passing techniques in the next chapter.

Catching the Corners

Cornering is important to race success. Getting into and out of each corner takes proper setup and control. Remember that your bike should lean much farther into the turn than your body.

1

1. As you approach the turn, keep your body weight centered between both wheels.

2

2. Lean the bike into the turn and keep your body angled upward, over the seat. Keep your outside pedal down to lower your center of gravity and make it easier to balance.

3

3. As you come through the turn, keep your hips, shoulders and head in the direction of the turn.

A Tip for Smooth Sailing

Whenever you're racing, you want to cut down wind resistance. If you're standing tall over your pedals, your body acts as a sail, catching the air and slowing your progress. So wherever you are on the track, don't give the air much to hold on to. Crouch down low over your seat, point your knees forward, and pedal like crazy!

If you're turning left, turn your body left to face the turn (right for right turns). Keep pedaling except at the tightest part of the turn. Sometimes a turn will be so sharp that you have to put down one foot to support yourself. In the BMX world that's called "hot-shoeing."

Chapter 4

Passing Techniques and Simple Tricks

There's no guarantee that you'll start out in first place in every race. In order to cross that finish line first after a slow start, you must learn how to pass. You can pass with raw speed, and you can also pass with strategy. It's best to use a combination of both. Riders pass when they get a good "line." A line refers to the rider's line of motion. In a race, you want to get a good line that limits the lines of other riders. There are many ways to pass in turns that limit the lines of other riders while shooting you into the lead.

Passing Maneuvers

You're riding hard in the middle of the pack, and you are now right behind the leader heading into the final turn. This is the final race of the day, and if you can pass him you take home the winner's trophy. How will you do it? Let's learn a few passing maneuvers to get things rolling.

Block Pass

A block pass is good if you are on the inside of a turn while the leader is on the outside of the turn. You want to block his line and move ahead of him as you exit the turn. The key in this move is establishing your position at the bottom of the berm.

1. As you come into the turn at the bottom of the berm, angle your bike upward so that you can cross the path of the leader on the upper side of the turn.

2. Pedal hard to the top of the turn. If you can get in front of the leader, he or she will have to slow down and you will take the lead.

Railing

Railing is the fastest way around a turn because you don't have to slow down at all. You will often move up a few spaces when you rail a turn.

1. As you spot the turn from behind the pack, set up to take the top of the berm.

2. Pedal hard as you rail around the top of the berm.

Be careful when railing when you're in the lead. Another rider can block your line with a block pass and leave you in the dust.

Slingshot

The slingshot is a good way to pass someone in a turn if he or she is riding on the middle or the outside of the berm.

1. Follow the front rider into the turn. Stay close, being careful not to touch the rider's back tire.

2. About halfway through the turn, shoot up to the top side of the turn and pedal hard.

3. As you rail the last part of the turn, you'll gain momentum and pass the other rider on the straightaway.

High-Low

The high-low is another way to pass a leader in the turns. This is a harder move to perfect, and it doesn't work as often as some of the other passing techniques described earlier.

1. As you head into the turn, start out on the high side.

2. If the leader moves to the high side to block your path, turn quickly toward the low side and zoom toward the inside of the turn. Just make sure that your front tire doesn't hit the leader's back tire as you shift from the high to the low side.

3. Time your move down low (make your move when the leader starts to move up high to block) so that you have the momentum advantage to get by quickly.

Race Hard—Be Safe

When learning racing strategies, you learn to cut people off and pass other bikes with only inches to spare. It's important to remember that it's never OK to risk your safety or the safety of other riders. Never cause another rider to crash. If you can't pass safely, don't do it. Keep looking for a better chance.

Protecting Your Lead

If you're in front of the pack, you want to stay there. What you have just learned about passing you must use in reverse to battle those trying to pass you. Protect your lead with a combination of skill and strategy. If you see someone trying to pass you in a turn, block the rider's line before he or she blocks yours. And, of course, pedal as fast as you can.

Other Tricks: Bunny Hop

The bunny hop is a good way to gain bike control skills.

1. Crouch down and prepare your body to spring the front tire up.

Bunny Hop (continued)

2. Spring up and lift the front wheel. As the front wheel rises, shift your weight back and lift your legs.

3. The entire bike will rise off the ground like a bunny. As you get stronger you will be able to jump higher off the ground.

Super Skid

Learn to really sling some dirt by practicing your skids. You'll use this skill when you cut a turn close in a race and need to maintain control of the bike. If possible, practice at the track or at a dirt field that has a similar feel.

1. Get up some speed and lean hard into a turn until you start to feel the rear wheel sliding out from under you.

2. Pull out of the skid by turning your handlebars in the direction of your skid. As your back wheel slides out to the right, turn your handlebars to the right to straighten yourself.

3. Come out of the super skid pedaling hard on the best line to the next obstacle or turn.

An Easy Air Trick

As you get the feel of your bike on jumps, you can start practicing some easy air tricks. You'll gain more control of your body and your bike, which will help you in all areas of racing.

1. Gain speed coming to a jump. Spot the top of the jump. This is where you'll launch from.

An Easy Air Trick (continued)

2. Spring off the top of the jump and fly into the air.

3. Push the back of your bike to the side with your feet.

4. Bring the wheels back in a straight line before you land.

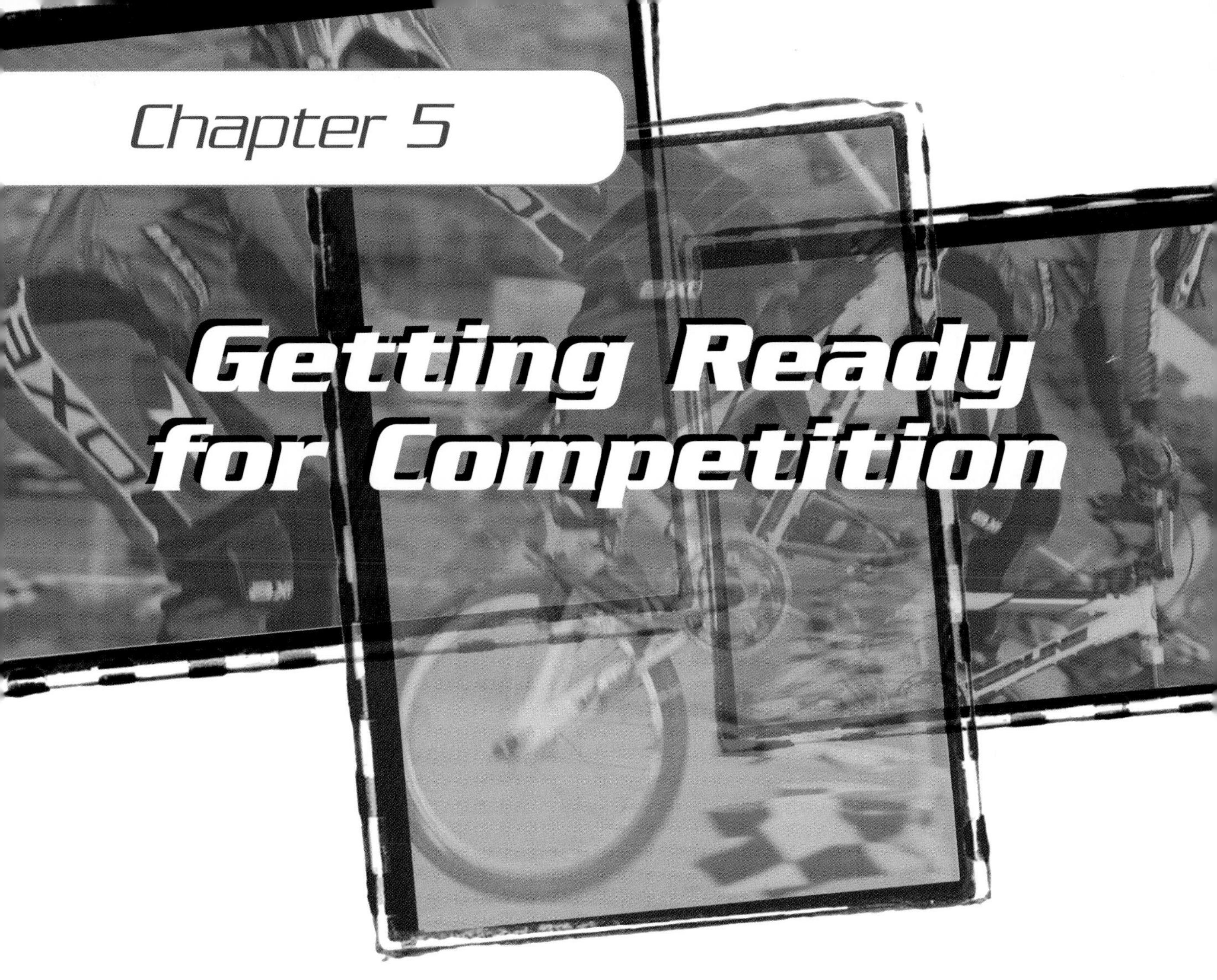

Chapter 5

Getting Ready for Competition

Knowledge means nothing without preparation in BMX. Practice makes perfect, and you'll have to prepare your body and your mind to be at their top form on race day. BMX riders must be in peak physical condition. You don't have to go to a fancy gym with workout machines. You've got your own workout machine already—your bike!

Ride for Exercise

The best way to get ready for races is to ride, ride, and ride some more. Ride sprints to increase your endurance. A sprint is a race over a short distance.

Mark a short distance and ride it as fast as you can. Then turn around and do it again. Time yourself with a stopwatch and see if your speed increases with practice. On other days take longer rides to increase your endurance. As a well-balanced athlete you want to be prepared for short bursts of speed and multiple-heat races on race day.

Mental Preparation

BMX is a tough physical sport, but it's just as important to train your mind for the competition. The best riders are those who block out all distractions and focus on the finish line. It's normal to get nervous before a race, but try calming your mind so you'll be sharp and ready to fly first through the gate when the starting signal sounds. See the race in your mind, and see yourself crossing the finish line. Before the race, take a few practice laps to get used to the track. Remember good places to pass and see yourself taking home the winner's cup.

What to Wear

The combination of high speed, dirt, tough jumps, and other riders on the track makes racing BMX dangerous. When you get suited up to ride in a BMX race, you protect your body from head to toe. You'll look like a knight in shining armor ready for battle—and that's what you are!

Even if you're just fooling around on the track before a race, make sure you protect your body. There are several essential pieces of safety equipment that every racer should wear. We'll start at the head first:

Helmet

Make sure you get a helmet that is designed for BMX racing. BMX helmets look a lot like motorcycle helmets. Many of them have mouth guards that wrap around and protect your entire face. There are a few different styles in

A full-face helmet *(left)* is essential for BMX racing safety. Notice that BMX helmets are larger and have more protection than a regular bicycle helmet. Riding pants *(right)* are made large to fit over knee pads and shin guards.

helmets, so you can shop around and see what works for you. Just make sure you're protected; don't worry about looking pretty for the cameras while you are racing.

Racing Leathers

You don't have to wear leather to race BMX, but leathers are great protection from burns on skidding falls. "Racing leathers" is the term used to describe the shirt and pants that protect you from dirt, scrapes, and falls. Some people wear jeans, while others wear special shirts and pants made out of nylon or other lightweight material. Cover any skin that is exposed on your arms and legs. When you fall, your arms and legs usually hit the ground first.

Your outfit should fit close to your body. Long-sleeve shirts with pads in the elbows will protect your arms. You can find special BMX shirts at your bike shop or order them over the Internet.

Make sure your pant legs can't get caught in the chain of your bike. That is a quick way to fall.

Elbow and forearm padding *(left)* should wrap around any areas that can suffer impact during a fall. Knee and shin guards *(right)* have thick foam padding beneath a hard plastic shell for added protection.

Elbow and Knee Pads/Shin Guards

Have you ever tried to pedal a bike with a skinned knee? It is not fun. If you don't have padded shirts or pants, put on elbow and knee pads. The first time you fall, you will be glad you were protected. And don't forget shin guards, which will protect your legs from spinning pedals.

Gloves

Racing gloves will protect your hands and will also serve as valuable cushions for rough riding and jumping. Buy full-finger gloves that go over the wrists. Most gloves are now heavily padded, and many use Kevlar fabric for better durability.

Shoes

Make sure you have durable shoes with a thick rubber sole on the bottom. Your shoes will absorb a lot of the impact on landings and will sometimes drag through the dirt in turns.

How to Fall

No amount of safety gear will prevent you from falling once in a while. No one likes to fall, especially when there are bikes flying through the air and whizzing by your head. But it does happen, and it pays to remember the one golden rule of falling: stay loose. If you stay relaxed when you fall, you are much more likely to bounce back up without injury. If you do hit the ground and there are other riders around you, get up quickly but do not run to the side if there are riders behind you. Make sure you are safe before trying to get back on your bike.

Buying shoes and gloves specially made for BMX racing is a good investment. They are durable for long-term use and padded for safety.

Injuries

Remember to respect your body if you want to race into the sunset after a long and fulfilling career. As in any sport, most injuries occur when people

Bike Maintenance: Taking Care of Your Ride

It pays to protect your body, and it also pays to protect your bike. Be sure to take care of your bike before and after every race. Look carefully at both wheels and examine the brake pads. Clean out any dirt that has gotten stuck in the brake pads, because that can make it harder to stop or brake in the turns. Make sure your chain is clean and oiled, too. Take your bike down to the shop for periodic tune-ups. If they'll let you, watch the bike mechanics as they check your ride. This way you'll know how to tune it up yourself.

are not paying attention to safety. Whenever you ride your bike, it is important to put safety first. If you're riding carelessly or trying to jump too high before learning control, you are running the risk of injury. In the world of freestyle BMX, it's not uncommon for a star to miss several months of competitions while he or she heals from an injury. It's hard to ride a bike when you're nursing a broken arm.

Safety is a serious issue at BMX tracks. Riders are not allowed to compete if they don't have appropriate equipment, and anyone who threatens the safety of other riders will be asked to exit the race.

Ready for Competition?

So now that you are itching to start, what do you do? Hopefully, there's a track in your town. The American Bicycling Association (ABA) and the National Bicycle League (NBL) are the two largest organizations that sponsor clubs and events across the country. Finding a track in your area can be as simple as logging on to the Internet. Try the ABA at www.ababmx.com and the NBL at www.nbl.org.

If there's a race in your area, you'll need to register and pay an entrance fee before hitting the track. If you're at a track sponsored by the ABA, you can get a temporary membership for about $25 that will last for about thirty days. This membership is necessary before you can race on the track. Make sure you have all the necessary safety equipment or else you might not be allowed to compete.

Sponsorships

You may dream of being a professional BMX racer. Just like any other sport, very few people make it to the professional level. But if you believe that you can make it as a BMX racer, you should follow your dream. Racers can take home as much as $10,000 for winning big events like the Vans Triple Crown.

Professional riders have sponsorships. This means that companies pay them to use certain products for free. That's a pretty good deal! The best way to get sponsored is to win a lot of races. Once you've made a name for yourself, you can approach a company and ask them if they want to sponsor you. National races like the ABA championships often have talent scouts who are looking for new riders to sponsor. Believe it—it can happen to you!

The Bumps and Berms of BMX

Once you're in the heat of a race, you'll need a combination of speed, power, skill, and strategy to come out on top. In this book, we've gone over some of the most important tools that every BMXer should have at his or her disposal. If you can keep these things in mind during every race, you'll always be a step ahead of the competition.

We've covered a lot of ground. This book should get you started and well on your way to winning the main. As you practice your skills, find some friends and ride together. Train your body and your mind.

BMX is a competitive sport, and everyone wants to be the best. But remember to ride for fun. The most rewarding effort is your own best effort.

Glossary

berm A banked turn on a BMX track.
cages Pedals that secure the rider's foot with a wraparound "cage."
clipless Pedals for advanced riders that attach the shoe to the pedal. These can be hard to remove in a fall.
hot-shoe Putting a foot down for support while riding through a turn.
line A rider's line of motion.
manual Pulling up the front wheel while pedaling the back wheel. This is an essential skill that enables you to power up jumps and learn bike control.
moto One lap around a BMX track.
roller One hill or jump on a BMX track.
step-up A small jump followed immediately by a larger one.
tabletop A jump with a flat surface between the front side and back side.
whoop-de-dos Several small hills, one after the other.

For More Information

American Bicycle Association-BMX (ABA-BMX)

P.O. Box 718
Chandler, AZ 85244
(480) 961-1903
http://www.ababmx.com/index3.html

National Bicycle League

3958 Brown Park Drive, Suite D
Hilliard, OH 43026
(800) 886-BMX1 (2691)

Web Sites

Due to the changing nature of Internet links, the Rosen Publishing Group, Inc., has developed an online list of Web sites related to the subject of this book. This site is updated regularly. Please use this link to access the list:

http://www.rosenlinks.com/rs/bmx/

For Further Reading

Alexander, Rod. *BMX Racing: A Step-by-Step Guide*. Memphis, TN: Troll Communications, 1990.

Carstensen, Karol. *BMX Bikes.* Mankato, MN: Capstone Press, 1991.

Dick, Scott. *BMX*. Crystal Lake, IL: Heinemann Library, 2002.

Gutman, Bill. *BMX Racing*. Mankato, MN: Capstone Press, 1995.

Herran, Joe and Ron Thomas. *BMX Riding*. Philadelphia: Chelsea House, 2002.

Nelson, Julie. *BMX Racing and Freestyle*. Austin, TX: Steck-Vaughn Publishers, 2002.

Bibliography

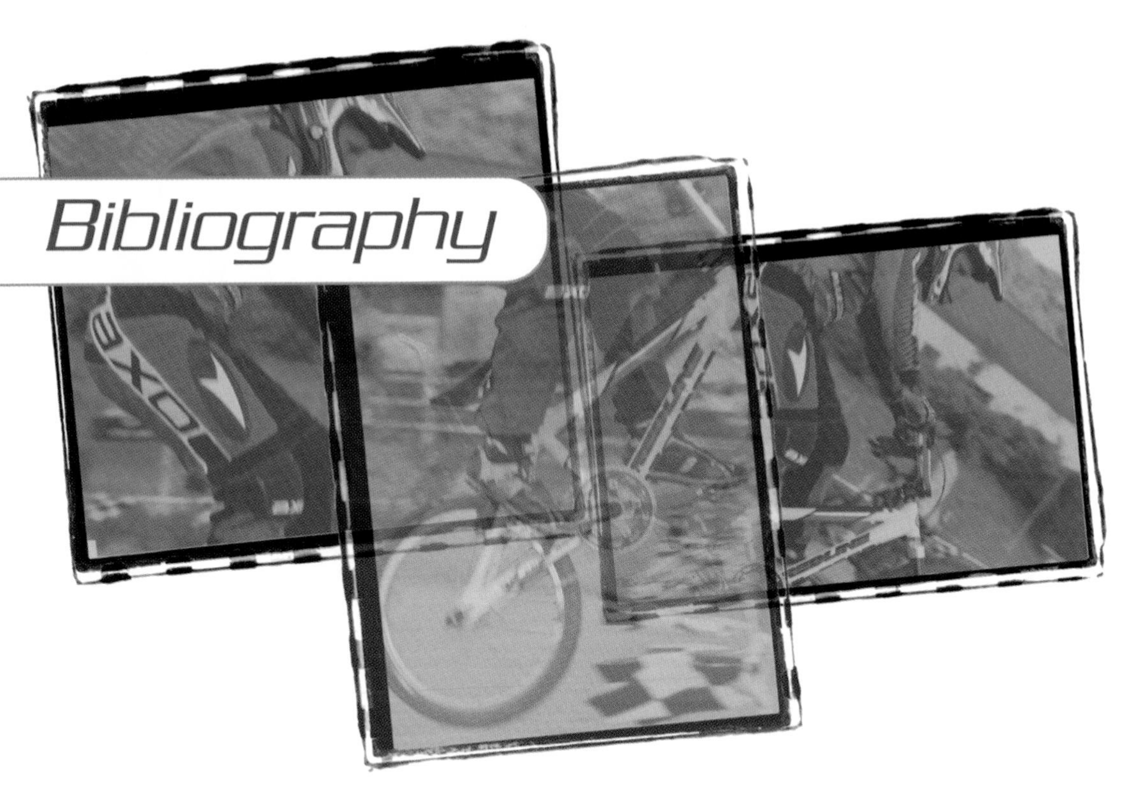

Alexander, Rod. *BMX Racing: A Step-by-Step Guide*. Memphis, TN: Troll Communications, 1990.

Boulais, Sue. *Learning How: BMX Biking.* Marco, FL: Bancroft-Sage Publishing, 1991.

Reisgies, Tess. "Get Into: BMX Racing." *Sports Illustrated for Kids*. February 1995, Vol. 7, issue 2, p. 50.

"Step by Step: An Instructional Video for BMX Racing." Produced by 101 Digital, XXX TV, and BMX Superstar. Videocassette. XXX Sports Multimedia, 1999.

"Triple Crown Pays Big." *RideBMX*. February 2002, Vol. 11, issue 2.

Index

P

R

S

T

W

About the Author

Brian Wingate still remembers his first BMX bike—a blue-and-white Mongoose. He also remembers his red-and-white BMX jersey with pads in the elbows. These days he lives in Tennessee and rides a mountain bike when he gets a chance.

Acknowledgments

Thanks to Harry Leary and to Marzocchi and Valencia BMX for providing the track.

Credits

Cover © AP/Wide World Photos; pp. 4–5 © Vince Streano/Corbis; pp. 7, 8, 10, 13–17, 19–22, 24, 27–34, 37–40 © Tony Donaldson/Icon SMI/Rosen Publishing; p. 23 © Lester Lefowitz/Corbis.

Editor

Mark Beyer

Design and Layout

Les Kanturek